Preparation of
ARCHIVAL COPIES
of Theses and Dissertations

Jane Boyd and Don Etherington

Physical Quality of Library Materials Committee
Resources and Technical Services Division
American Library Association

American Library Association
CHICAGO AND LONDON
1986

Text composed by Jaymes Anne Rohrer
in Madeleine PS on a Tandy 2000
Personal Computer. Display type,
Weiss Roman, composed by Pearson
Typographers.

Printed on Warren's 1854, a
pH-neutral stock, and bound in
65# Sunray cover stock by
the University of Chicago
Printing Department

Library of Congress Cataloging-in-Publication Data

Boyd, Jane.
    Preparation of archival copies of theses and
dissertations.

    1. Library materials—Conservation and restoration—
Standards. 2. Dissertations, Academic--Conservation
and restoration--Standards.   I. Etherington, Don.
II. American Library Association.   Physical Quality
of Library Materials Committee.   III. Title.
Z701.B79   1986   025.7   85-28939
ISBN 0-8389-0449-1

Contents

Preface

These guidelines have been written to assist institutions in setting requirements for the preparation of an archival copy of a thesis or dissertation. They address issues such as the best method for mounting photographs in a bound volume, use of adhesives which will be safe and yet permanent, and the best duplication methods. In the interest of brevity and simplicity, we refer only to "thesis," but "thesis or dissertation" is implied throughout. Individual institutions should adapt these guidelines to fit their own specific requirements.

Preparation of Archival Copies of Theses and Dissertations was written at the suggestion and sponsorship of the Physical Quality of Library Materials Committee, of which Don Etherington was a member. The committee is a subgroup of Resources and Technical Services Division of the American Library Association.

I. PAPER QUALITY

A. Archival Copy

The thesis must either be typed or printed on high-quality, durable, white paper, $8\frac{1}{2}$ x 11 inches in size and at least 20-pound weight. (For material larger than this, see "Oversized Material.") The paper chosen for the archival copy of the thesis must be selected for its permanence and durability and must be acid-free with a minimum of 2 percent alkaline reserve. (For sources of paper, see Section XIV.)

Erasable papers (sometimes called Corrasable) lack absorbent qualities. Any typing done on this kind of paper will be permanently subject to smudging. This paper is, therefore, not acceptable for any part of the thesis.

B. Copies (See also "Duplication")

Copies of the thesis should also be on an acid-free paper with a 2 percent alkaline reserve, again with a minimum weight of 20 pounds. Papers with high rag content do not work well in electrostatic or xerographic copy machines. If papers containing cotton rag are used in this type of copy machine, the rag content should not exceed 25 percent. When there is a higher rag content, the copied image can easily be erased or rubbed off.[1]

---

1. Harvard University, "The Form of the Doctoral Thesis" (a supplement to the Graduate School of Arts and Sciences Handbook) (Cambridge, Mass.: The University, 1984), 7.

II. TYPING

Any easily readable standard type in pica or elite measure is acceptable.[2] Typing should be on only one side of the paper. All textual material should be double-spaced but long quotations and footnotes may be single-spaced. It is preferable to use the same typewriter for the entire thesis to ensure a uniform appearance.

Examples, quotations, tables, etc., may be accentuated and set off from the rest of the text by using different typefaces. However, all typefaces used should be of similar size and easily legible. The body of the thesis may be written in a different size typeface than the footnotes, section headings, and chapter titles, but these must also be very legible and no smaller than elite type. Type produced on a dot-matrix printer must have a resolution of more than 200 dots per inch to be acceptable. Script type is not acceptable.

The type on the typewriter should be cleaned and well maintained to ensure consistent clear printing. A black typewriter ribbon should be used, preferably film or nylon. An inked ribbon should be changed often enough to ensure dark, even impressions. The very dark cloth ribbons are more likely to smudge, especially when they are new.

There are certain symbols not available on typewriters (such as subscripts, mathematical symbols, exponents, etc.) which may have to be neatly hand printed using permanent black ink (e.g., India ink, Koh-i-noor rapidograph waterproof drawing ink, etc.). Permission to include such symbols is generally granted by the supervising professor.

III. MARGINS

The margins for the text of the thesis should be approximately 1 inch at the top, bottom and right side, and $1\frac{1}{2}$ inches on the left side of the page. The extra $\frac{1}{2}$ inch on the left is to allow for binding. This same $1\frac{1}{2}$-inch binding allowance should be made on the appropriate side if the paper is turned 90 degrees in the typewriter when typing tables, charts, or other similar material.

As an aid for measuring top and bottom margins, one inch

---

2. Standard typewriter spacing is six vertical spaces to an inch. Pica type has ten characters in a horizontal inch; elite type has twelve characters in a horizontal inch.

equals six typewriter lines, and for measuring side margins, one inch equals twelve elite or ten pica spaces.

All information including titles, footnotes and illustrations must conform to the margins specified (except for page numbers). Large plates, charts, etc., must be reduced when possible so that they fit within the prescribed margins, but any notations or writing on them must be easily legible and no smaller than elite type. When plates larger than $8\frac{1}{2}$ x 11 inches cannot be reduced, refer to the section entitled "Oversized Material" for directions.

Beginning major sections of the thesis on a new page may avoid some retyping. Using pencilled page numbers until the thesis is entirely approved may save time and some tedious revisions. The final page numbers can then be inserted using the typewriter after all changes have been made. This procedure will be especially helpful when illustrative material will be interleaved with the text.

IV. CORRECTIONS

Corrections of typographical errors, other than by clean erasure and by certain self-correcting typewriters, are not acceptable. Any corrections must be made with care since unsightly corrections or changes which are unlikely to reproduce clearly on microfilm are unacceptable. Correction fluid should not be used on any archival copy to be submitted because it damages the paper and occasionally bleeds or flakes away from the paper, exposing the uncorrected type. Correction fluid also appears as a different shade from the paper color in the microfilm copy and is therefore distracting and unsightly.

Self-correcting typewriters like the IBM Selectric and the Royal SE 5000 CD/C may be used to correct errors if it is done carefully and neatly. Typewriters which use correcting tape to "cover up" errors should not be used.

Any corrections needed should be made on the original before it is photocopied. Corrections on photocopies to be submitted are not acceptable.

V. ILLUSTRATIONS

It is common in many areas of study for a thesis to include illustrations. These may be reproductions of works of art, line drawings, facsimiles of manuscript pages, photographs (see also "Photographs"), graphs, maps, chemical formulas, computer printouts, or musical scores. Any original illustrative material to be submitted should be rendered with a permanent, non-water soluble, black ink (e.g., India ink, Koh-i-noor rapidograph waterproof drawing ink, etc.). The use of pencil is not acceptable on the original, nor is the use of felt-tip pen since the color bleeds through to the adjacent pages. The use of color, especially in graphs, charts or maps, should be avoided because colors often cannot be distinguished in microfilm copies. Since microfilm is a black-and-white photographic process, colors tend to appear as slightly differing shades of gray. Therefore, lines of a graph should be identified using symbols or labels instead of colors. Areas on maps may be indicated by cross-hatching rather than by color.

All illustrations must be produced on quality paper, the minimum standards for which are specified under "Paper Quality." Charts and graphs on transparent film or illustrations produced by computers on lower quality paper must be photocopied on quality paper (see "Paper Quality--Copies" and "Duplication").

Small illustrations must be mounted by one of the following methods. The first is the dry-mount process. With this method, dry-mount tissue (made by Kodak and others), placed between the illustration and the mounting paper, fuses when heat is applied (either by a heat press or an electric iron).

Another method, involving the use of a cold-mount adhesive called "Positionable Mount Adhesive" (Scotch Brand No. 568), may be more convenient since it does not require heat for adhesion. Due to its "bubble" construction, the adhesive film forms a strong bond only after it has been pressed firmly. Illustrations may therefore be picked up and repositioned if necessary. Also, because the adhesive film is so thin, there will be no problem with shadows around the edges of an illustration after it is mounted.

Rubber cement, aerosol spray glues, and gummed or cellophane tapes deteriorate rapidly and therefore should not be used for mounting illustrations. Spray adhesives and dry-mount cements should not be used because, in time, they are likely to produce chemical spotting of the print or to pull away from the mounting sheet.

When many smaller illustrations are used throughout the thesis, it is advisable to distribute the bulk by placing a portion of the illustrations toward the top of the page and the rest toward the bottom in order to even out the thickness of the book.

When smaller illustrations are being mounted using one of the above methods, it is important to have page numbers and identification of figures already typed on the mounting paper. This information should be typed either beneath the figure or on the front of the preceding page. Avoid typing information on the back of the preceding page (facing the illustration) because the information might be overlooked when the microfilm copy is made. Figures and tables should be numbered either by chapter or in sequence throughout the thesis.

Large charts, tables, figures, etc., which must be reduced to fit within the prescribed margins must have lettering and symbols which, after reduction, are at least as large as elite type so that they can be read easily.

A small figure or table may be included on a text page in its logical location. Larger illustrations are usually on a separate following page. If there are several illustrations or more than a page or two of illustrations, and inserting them in the text would be unnecessarily distracting, they may follow the text of the thesis in an appendix. However, since most theses will be read in microfilm, it is important to place tables and illustrations as near to the pertinent text as possible. Page numbers should be given to illustrations which are interleaved with the text.

VI. PHOTOGRAPHS

Only black-and-white photographs should be submitted with the thesis. Photographs copied by photocopy machines are unacceptable. Ideally, there should be a wide range of contrast within each photograph from true black to pure white. This is preferred because although photographs without a wide range of contrast can be reproduced successfully on positive microfilm, they will not be clear in photostatic copies made from the microfilm. If a color photograph is necessary and must be used, a photograph of the same subject in black and white should be included since color photographs tend to fade. The photographs included in the archival copy of the thesis should receive archival processing if possible.

A high standard of archival processing of photographs is specified by the American National Standards Institute (ANSI). These standards are listed under the following ANSI numbers: PH 4.29, PH 4.30, PH 4.32, and PH 4.33. In some cities it will not be possible to meet this standard of archival processing. In this case, request the best available processing.

Photographs should be printed on an $8\frac{1}{2}$-x-11-inch sheet of light-weight or single-weight polyfiber photographic paper with a glossy finish and included in the thesis without further mounting. The margins for the photographic image should be the same as those for typing (see "Margins"). If the 8½-x-11-inch size paper is not available, have the photograph(s) printed on a larger paper of this specific type and trim to size. This type of paper in 8-x-10-inch size may be used if the larger size cannot be found.

If the photographs are less than 8½ x 11 inches, the following techniques should be considered: (1) photographs may be photoreproduced or photo-offset if the tonal values and quality of the photograph are maintained and the photograph remains suitable for further reproduction; (2) original photographs may be dry mounted, on heavier weight paper if possible (approximately 80 pound); (3) photographs may also be mounted using the cold-mount material Positionable Mount Adhesive #568 discussed in the section "Illustrations." This material does not require heat for adhesion.

No other adhesive should be used. Rubber cement, gummed or cellophane tapes should not be used for mounting since these materials deteriorate rapidly. Spray adhesives and dry-mount cements should not be used either because, in time, they are likely to produce chemical spotting of the print or to pull away from the mounting sheet. Photographic corners and acetate pockets are not acceptable for mounting because they often damage the corners of the photograph.

The dry-mounting process is a good mounting method. It employs a special photographic tissue which, when placed between the illustration and the mounting surface, will fuse when heat is applied either by a heat press or an electric iron. Dry-mount tissue is made by Kodak as well as other companies. Positionable Mount Adhesive #568 is another good mounting material, as discussed earlier.

Problems encountered when mounting photographs in a bound volume will be solved by having photographs printed on the proper fiberbase paper with the margins adjusted so that they will be the appropriate size for the thesis.

When possible, mounted photographs should not extend into the 1½-inch binding margin on the left side of the thesis.

When a number of smaller photographs are used as illustrations throughout the thesis, it would be advisable to distribute the bulk by placing a portion of the photographs toward the top of the page and the rest toward the bottom in order to even out the thickness of the book.

VII. OVERSIZED MATERIAL

Occasional exceptions to the 8½-x-11-inch paper size

limitation are made when deemed necessary, as is sometimes the case with musical scores. The same physical specifications as listed under "Paper Quality" must be applied to all oversized material included in a thesis.

Charts, maps, graphs, tables, or any other necessary illustrative material which is larger than the standard page size and cannot be successfully reduced may be carefully folded and included in order in the thesis or stored in a large acid-free envelope or pocket attached to the back board of the cover of the thesis. Oversized material to be stored in an envelope should be folded so that it is approximately 1 inch narrower than the width of the envelope and about 1/8 of an inch shorter than the length of the envelope. For example: the dimensions of the envelope are 7 1/2 x 10 inches. The outer dimensions of the folded oversized material to be stored should be no larger than 6 1/2 x 9 7/8 inches. These envelopes can be obtained in acid-free material from a number of sources. (For a list of sources, see Section XIV.)

It should be noted that such oversized pages complicate microfilming the thesis and should be avoided whenever possible. When oversized pages are microfilmed, they often must be done in several separate frames, which may mean a loss in continuity.

When oversized material is to be included in order as a regular page in the thesis, the illustrative material should be arranged on the page to allow a margin of $1\frac{1}{2}$ inches on the binding edge. When the illustration is folded, this binding margin must protrude from the folds and be a $1\frac{1}{2}$-inch stub on the left side of the folded illustration. This stub is shown in figure 1, a diagram of a large page with marks where folds are to be made and the binding margin indicated.[3] The illustration should be folded carefully so that there are as few folds made as possible, and so that the page can be easily unfolded after the thesis is bound. The folded outer edges of the illustration should be $\frac{1}{2}$ inch smaller than the text pages on all three unbound edges of the thesis. The overall dimensions of the folded illustration, then, will be approximately 8 x 10 inches. With these dimensions the bindery can safely trim 1/8 inch off the three open edges of the thesis without slicing into the folds.

---

3. Rensselaer Polytechnic Institute, Thesis Writing--Manual for Master's and Doctor's Theses (Troy, New York: The Institute, 1983), 35.

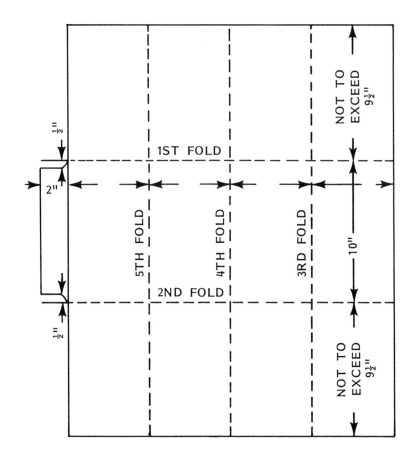

Figure 1. Oversized page with folds and binding margin indicated.

VIII. DUPLICATION

Photocopying is a good method of duplication, but copy quality must be extremely good. This standard of quality is possible only if the machine used is very clean and well maintained. Copies with stray marks, smudges, or other irregularities will not be accepted. The image must be tested for smudging (by attempting erasure) to make sure that the machine is in good operating condition, even if it has a good reputation for copy permanence.

The electrostatic method of photoduplication, which uses dry toner and a fusing technique with heat and pressure, is good. Duplication methods which use papers coated with an image-forming layer are not acceptable, nor are those which use processes involving zinc oxide. It is important that the electrostatic copier be properly adjusted. Smudges on freshly made copy indicate that the machine is not fusing properly. It must be readjusted and the smudging problem corrected before copying is resumed.

Photocopies should have consistently dark print quality with high contrast throughout the thesis. Any copies which appear significantly lighter than the rest must be recopied to conform to a uniform dark, clear print quality.

It should be noted that photocopy machines enlarge the original by approximately 1 percent. This varies slightly among different machines, but it is important to be aware of this enlargement so that margin limitations will not be exceeded.

Maps, charts, figures, and other illustrations may be reduced on reduction photocopy machines provided that any accompanying text does not become smaller than the typeface of the text or than elite type. Each copy of the thesis should be carefully collated.

IX. THESIS PREPARATION ON A COMPUTER

The preparation of a thesis by text-processing techniques has many advantages. The text can be easily revised and the layout readily controlled and adjusted. From the rough drafts to the final copy, all revisions are easily printed and the amount of proofreading needed is greatly reduced compared to typing each version again. The time and effort involved in learning to use computers and text-processing techniques seems to be well spent considering the great reduction of time spent retyping and proofreading. Duplication of the thesis can also be done easily by having the computer print more copies rather than having them photocopied. A thesis produced by computer is, of course, subject to all the same requirements as any other thesis, such as paper quality, typing, type quality, margins, etc. (See Section XIV for sources of paper.)

X. COMPUTER PRINTOUTS

A computer printout to be submitted as part of the thesis should be reduced to the standard $8\frac{1}{2}$-x-11-inch page size. Computer paper which is 11 x 14 7/8 reduces to $8\frac{1}{2}$ x 11 inches after a 77 percent reduction by photocopy machine. Margin requirements are the same as for the rest of the thesis. The reduced print cannot be smaller than elite type and should be of dark, clear, good quality. Computer printouts used in the main text of the thesis must meet the standards specified for paper quality and must have printing which is dark and legible so that it can be reproduced on microfilm. If the available printer does not produce clear print, the computer printout should be typed.

XI.   MUSIC AND RECORDED SOUND

The best commonly available method of storing recorded sound is recording on reel-to-reel magnetic tape which has 1.5-mil polyester or Mylar backing.[4] This type of tape is relatively free of inherent vice and is not easily damaged, short of gross abuse. For archival storage a high performance grade tape is recommended which must be 1.5-mil polyester or Mylar based, with low noise and high output. The following brands are generally reliable and of good quality: Ampex, AGFA, Scotch (3M), TDK, BASF, and Maxell. In order to be long-lasting, tape should be stored under proper conditions.

Maintaining correct winding tension is one essential aspect of proper use and storage of tapes. The tape machine keeps the tape under tension while it is being played so that it will move onto and off the storage reels smoothly and will wind evenly. The tape, therefore, is designed to withstand being wound under tension and stored under tension without suffering any deformation. A tape may be damaged, however, if normal tension is exceeded. Such damage can mean distortion or loss of sound. Insufficient tension can damage tapes as well. Therefore, correct winding tension, controlled mainly by the tape machine being used, must be maintained for proper storage and use of tapes.

A tape that is to be stored should be wound on a storage reel at normal forward speed, not at higher speeds used for fast-forward or rewind. Tapes should be stored after they have been played without being rewound. This is commonly known as "tails out" storage because the end of the tape is left outside the reel.

---

4. This entire section on music and recorded sound is adapted from Jerry McWilliams' book, The Preservation and Restoration of Sound Recordings (Nashville: American Assn. for State and Local History Pr., 1979).

A. Acid-free Paper

1. Archival Copy (Typing paper)

Conservation Materials
Ltd.
240 Freeport Blvd.
Sparks, NV 89431
(702) 331-0582
Product name: Permalife

Fox River Paper Co.
P.O. Box 2215
Appleton, WI 54911
Product name: Fox River
Bond

University Products, Inc.
P.O. Box 101
Holyoke, MA 01040
(413) 532-9431/532-4272
Product name: Perma-Dur

Crane and Company
Dalton, MA 01226
Product name: Crane's
Thesis Bond

2. Photocopy

Xerox
For orders in any region:
1-800-822-2200
Product name: Xerox
XXV Archival Bond

3. Computer Printout

Conservation Materials,
Ltd.
240 Freeport Blvd.
Sparks, NV 89431
(702) 331-0582
Product name: Permalife

Jerome Business Forms,
Inc.
20 Millpark Court
Maryland Heights, MD 63043
(314) 428-7799

B. Acid-free Envelopes

Conservation Resources
International
1111 N. Royal St.
Alexandria, VA 22314
(703) 549-6610

Process Materials Corp.
P.O. Box 368
Rutherford, NJ 07070
(201) 935-2900

Hollinger Corporation
P.O. Box 6185
Arlington, VA 22206
(703) 671-6600

University Products, Inc.
P.O. Box 101
Holyoke, MA 01040
(413) 532-9431/532-4272

C. Mounting Adhesive

3M Company
For orders in any region:
1-800-442-8046

Product name: Scotch
Brand Tape No. 568

Don Etherington is chief conservation officer at the Harry Ransom Humanities Research Center at the University of Texas at Austin.

Jane Boyd formerly was assistant book conservator at the Harry Ransom Humanities Research Center at the University of Texas at Austin.